"BREACH OF THE RULES"

KENNETH BROWN

PUBLISHER

Lulu.com

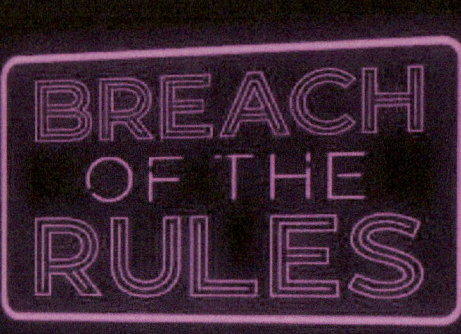

BREACH OF THE RULES

KENNETH A. BROWN

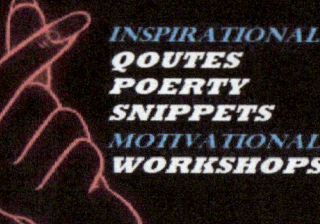

INSPIRATIONAL
QOUTES
POERTY
SNIPPETS
MOTIVATIONAL
WORKSHOPS

ISBN: 978-1-4583-7016-7
Imprint: Lulu.com

Dedication

Lord Jesus thank you for guiding me and allowing me to follow you on this journey called life. You have tested my strength, my heart, my will, and my ability to remain sane. But I was and am ok with that because I know you are only making me a stronger soldier for your battle. I want to thank my family and friends for my inspiration. Thank you to all my loyal readers.

Table of Contents

BREACH OF THE RULES

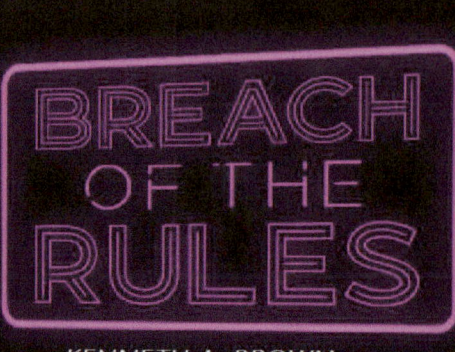

KENNETH A. BROWN

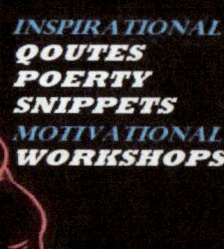

INSPIRATIONAL
QOUTES
POERTY
SNIPPETS
MOTIVATIONAL
WORKSHOPS

INTRODUCTION

"Life can feel overwhelming when we're stuck in survival mode or reacting without pause. A workshop on honoring life's guiding rules; like boundaries, respect, and emotional honesty can offer the clarity and tools to navigate everyday problems with more confidence, calm, and connection."

We live by rules we never choose.

Some are spoken— "Don't cry," "Be strong," "Fit in."
Others are silent but deeply rooted—rules about who we're allowed to be, what we're allowed to feel, and how much of ourselves we're allowed to show.

These rules were often born in childhood, shaped by fear, shame, or survival. But while they may have protected us once, they now limit us. They keep us disconnected from our truth, our emotions, and the people we long to be close to.

This book is about breaking those rules.

Not the rules that keep us safe—but the ones that keep us small. The ones that silence our voice, suppress our joy, and hide our wounds. It's about healing what's hidden, reclaiming what's real, and stepping into the life you were always meant to live.

Through reflection, stories, and practical guidance, you'll learn how to meet yourself with compassion, connect more deeply with others, and live with the kind of emotional freedom that only comes when we stop apologizing for who we are.

Your healing starts here.
Your freedom is not found in perfection—
It's found in breaking the right rules.

QUESTIONS

Name:

Age:

What's Your zodiac sign?

What do you do for a living?

Does salary matter in a relationship? Yes or No.

Do you have kids?

Do you want kids?

Have you ever been married?

Do you want to get married?

Are you currently single?

What kind of relationship are you looking for? (Polyamorous, Monogamous, Triad etc.).

What kind of person do you desire, prefer or look for?

Do you have any deal breakers?

Do you have an appearance requirement, do the person have to look a certain way?

Do the person have to make a certain amount of money?

When was your last relationship?

Why couldn't you be with that person?

Why would someone be lucky to be with you?

Do you prefer to chase the person or be courted?

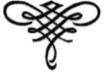

Premium

Workshop Chapter 1: "Letting Go – Breaking Rules, Finding Peace"

Workshop Chapter 1: "Letting Go – Breaking Rules, Finding Peace"

Introduction:

We've all broken a few rules in life—not just the ones written in books, but the ones society places on who we're supposed to be, how we should act, and what our journey should look like. But here's the truth:

Sometimes breaking the rules is what saves us. It teaches us who we are, what we need, and what we're no longer willing to tolerate.

🧠 Lesson: Letting Go Isn't Weakness—It's Wisdom

You can't change your past. You can't rewrite the decisions, the pain, or the chaos. But you can choose to stop carrying them like chains.

Letting go to it isn't about pretending it didn't happen.
It's about saying:
"Yes, it happened." And I'm still here. But I don't need to relive it anymore."

🛠️ Workshop Exercise: Release & Reset

1. **Write down 3 rules you were taught that limited you.**
   (Example: "Real men don't cry" / "You'll never be good enough")
2. **Next to each one, write how breaking it led to growth.**
   ("I cried—and it made me feel stronger.")

3. **Now write a short letter to your past self**-forgiving them for surviving the only way they knew how.

_____

_____

✦ **Closing Thought:**

You're not defined by your mistakes. You're defined by what you do with them. So, breathe. Let go. And take your next step to be free. Your past hurt can affect your future relationships. Holding on to the past prevents you from moving on in life. While it is great to appreciate your past positive or bad experiences and learn from your mistakes. It does create limitations in people's lives and set boundaries for the future.

So, embrace the unknown. Give yourself permission to let go. Because of your trust issues, it may be your number one obstacle to real love connection & experiencing real intimacy. And remember, there cannot be intimacy without love or there cannot be love without intimacy. No matter your situation, if you are feeling as though your relationship is lacking on the love side of things, perhaps then it is necessary to create more intimacy through physical connections, as intimacy is a key to unlocking and freeing any held back feelings of love. I get it, after being hurt from our past relationships, we fear being hurt again. We are reluctant to take on another chance at being loved.

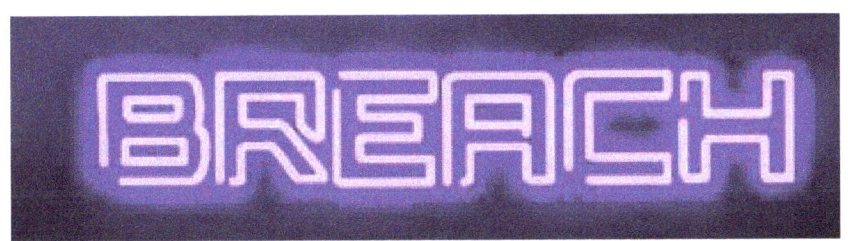

I am not crazy. I am not giving into these psychotic and evil bitches. I am not giving them what they want. Truth is before you diagnose yourself with depression or low self-esteem. First make sure that you are not, in fact just surrounded by assholes. Deception and lies shatter the reality of others, eroding their belief in the veracity of their perception and subjective experience. But if you're lucky you may find your soulmate, it all depends on you.

the Weekly
JOURNAL

Workshop Chapter 2: "Communicating Effectively – Breaking Silence, Building Connection"

Workshop Chapter 2: "Communicating Effectively – Breaking Silence, Building Connection"

Introduction:

Sometimes, we grow up learning how to **hide our truth**, to stay silent, to suppress what we feel just to keep the peace. We're told "don't say too much," "don't rock the boat," or "keep it to yourself." But what if real growth comes from **breaking those unspoken rules**?

Effective communication is not weakness—it's power.
Whether you're single, in a relationship, or facing family tension, your voice is your tool. Use it.

💬 The Power of Speaking Up

When you communicate clearly and honestly:

- You stop assuming and start understanding.
- You stop bottling up resentment and start building peace.
- You stop performing for approval and start honoring your truth.

💡 Being Single:

- Communicate your **boundaries and expectations** early in dating.
- Use solitude to practice **self-reflection** and learn how to express your needs clearly.
- Break the rule that says, *"You have to settle to be loved."*

Affirmation: "I don't shrink to be chosen. I speak up to be respected."

💕 In Relationships:

- Replace silence with vulnerability—say what hurts, what heals, and what you hope for.
- Practice **active listening**—don't just hear, *understand*.
- Break the rule that says, *"You have to fight to be heard."* Try clarity instead of conflict.

Mantra: "I communicate not to win, but to connect."

🏠 With Family:

- Speak from a place of love—but with **firmness and honesty**.
- Let go of trying to please everyone. Communicating your boundaries is an act of self-care.
- Break the rule that says, *"Family can treat you any way they want."*

Reflection: You can love them and still teach them how to treat you.

📝 Workshop Exercise: Real Talk Practice

1. **Identify a current situation** where you feel misunderstood or silent.
2. Write down:
   - What you *wish* you could say.
   - What's *stopping* you?

○   How would it feel to release that truth—peaceful? Scary? Empowering?

3.   Draft a simple, calm message to open the conversation.

✦ **Closing Thought:**

Your words are your freedom.
Break the rule that tells you to stay silent and suffer. Whether single, partnered, or dealing with family—**clarity heals.** Speak with truth, speak with love, and never apologize for honoring your voice.

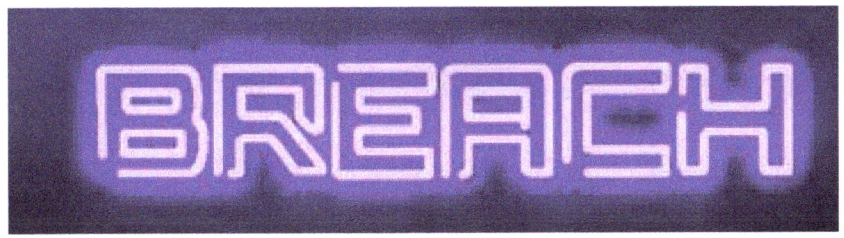

I did not stop checking on you because I stopped caring. I stop checking on you because you showed me absolutely no effort that you are interested. It is time to face the facts and move on.

the Weekly JOURNAL

Workshop Chapter 3: "Master Your Immaturity – Breaking the Rules to Grow Without Shame"

Workshop Chapter 3: "Master Your Immaturity – Breaking the Rules to Grow Without Shame"

Introduction:

We all carry parts of ourselves that haven't fully grown up—parts that pout, sabotage, overreact, avoid, or shut down. Society tells us to **hide** these parts or feel ashamed of them. But growth doesn't happen through hiding—it happens through honesty.

Mastering your immaturity doesn't mean being perfect. It means facing your patterns with love, not judgment.

When you stop pretending you've got it all together, you finally make space to grow.

⬤ **Rules That Keep You Emotionally Stuck**

Society says:

- "Don't admit your flaws—it makes you weak."
- "Act like you're okay, even when you're not."
- "Mature people don't feel jealousy, insecurity, or fear."
- "You're too old to still be acting like that."

But here's the truth:

- Immaturity is a human experience, not a permanent label.
- Pretending to be okay keeps you from becoming okay.
- Growth begins with truth, not image.
- There's no age limit on healing childhood wounds.

🌱 How Mastering Your Immaturity Helps You Thrive

When You're Single:

- You stop blaming others and start owning your patterns.
- You heal the part that chases validation or avoids intimacy.
- You prepare for healthier love by becoming emotionally available to yourself.

In a Relationship:

- You respond instead of reacting.
- You communicate with clarity, not control.
- You stop expecting your partner to "fix" your insecurities and learn how to soothe yourself.

With Family:

- You stop repeating generational emotional habits.
- You hold space for your inner child—without letting them drive the whole relationship.
- You stop playing roles (the fixer, the rebel, the pleaser) and show up as your true self.

🧠 Signs of Unacknowledged Immaturity

- You shut down when you don't get your way.
- You use silence or sarcasm instead of honest communication.
- You expect others to guess your needs.
- You get triggered by boundaries or accountability.

🛠️ How to Master (Not Deny) Your Immaturity

1. **Identify Your Default Coping Style**
   Do you withdraw? Blame? Over-apologize? Name the pattern without shame.
2. **Give Your Inner Child a Voice, Not the Wheel**
   Let them express—but then let your adult self-lead the response.
3. **Practice Response Over Reaction**
   Take 10 seconds before reacting. Ask: "Am I responding as my current self—or my hurt self?"
4. **Celebrate Progress, Not Perfection**
   Every time you choose growth over defense, you're winning.

 Workshop Exercise: Dialogue with Your Immature Self

Part 1: Journal Prompts

- What behavior or reaction am I ashamed to admit?
- When did I first learn to cope this way?
- What would it feel like to meet this version of me with compassion?

Part 2: Inner Dialogue
Write a short conversation between your mature self and your immature self. Let one listen, and the other express.

Example:
Immature Self: "I feel ignored and unloved."
Mature Self: "That makes sense. I'm here now. We can choose differently."

Affirmation:

"I am not ashamed of my past reactions.
I honor the younger version of me that did what they knew.
Today, I lead myself with compassion, not criticism.
I grow—without guilt."

⬭ Closing Thought:

Emotional immaturity isn't proof you're broken.
It's proof you're still healing.
When you stop hiding the messy parts of you and start listening to them,
you gain wisdom, strength, and emotional power.

You don't need to be perfect to be ready.
You just need to be honest to begin.

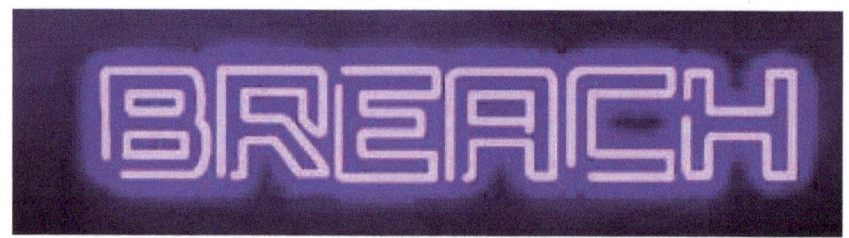

"Growing up doesn't mean pretending to have it all together—it means breaking the rules that shame you for still learning, still feeling, still fumbling. Mastering your immaturity is about embracing your humanity, owning your growth, and evolving without apology.

the Weekly
JOURNAL

Workshop Chapter 4: "Speaking Your Truth – Breaking the Silence to Build Real Connection"

Workshop Chapter 4: "Speaking Your Truth – Breaking the Silence to Build Real Connection"

Introduction:

From an early age, many of us are taught to **hold it in**to being quiet, agreeable, or "strong" by keeping our feelings to ourselves. We're told that honesty makes things messy, that speaking up might push people away.

But here's the truth: **the real disconnection comes from silence, not speech.**
Breaking the rules of silence is how we build authentic bonds. **Speaking your truth isn't rebellion—it's self-respect.**

🗣 Why Speaking Your Truth Matters

When you express your real feelings, fears, and desires:

- You give others **permission** to be honest too.
- You create **emotional safety** and trust.
- You stop carrying the weight of unspoken pain.

Truth is the bridge between misunderstanding and connection.

💡 Truth in Action: Emotional-Level Communication

Whether with a partner, a friend, or a family member, deep connection starts with:

- **Clarity**: Say what you mean without sugarcoating or attacking.
- **Courage**: Say it even if your voice shakes.
- **Compassion**: Speak from your heart, not your wounds.

Examples:

- "I feel unheard when you talk over me. I want us to understand each other better."
- "I'm scared to be vulnerable, but I value this relationship too much to stay silent."

▶ When You Don't Speak Your Truth:

- Resentment builds.
- Relationships become surface-level.
- You disconnect from your *own* emotions.
- You start to feel invisible—even around people you love.

📝 Workshop Exercise: Heart Talk Journal

1. Think of one person you want to connect with more deeply.
2. Write:
   - What truth have I been afraid to say?
   - What emotion am I hiding behind (anger, fear, guilt)?
   - What would I say if I believed they would truly listen?
3. Turn that into a simple, honest statement and practice saying it aloud to yourself.

✦ Affirmation:

"My truth matters. I don't have to yell at it to make it real. I just have to say it—with honesty, love, and strength."

⬭ **Closing Thought:**

Speaking your truth is one of the boldest forms of healing. It breaks the rules of pretending, pleasing, and performing.
It opens the door to **real connection**, the kind built not on perfection—but on truth.

"Connection doesn't come from who we pretend to be. It comes from who we're brave enough to be."

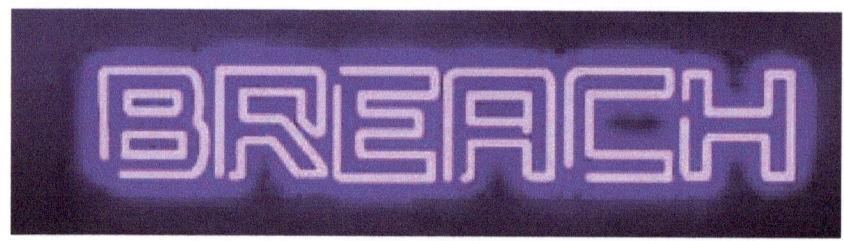

The Truth is, we must start letting the other person know that their behavior is affecting us and propose a possible solution. But if they continue to make the same mistakes with poor choices. Then you should no longer offer love, hope, & reassurance. You should move on.

the Weekly

JOURNAL

Workshop Chapter 5: "Spiritual Rebirth – Breaking the Rules to Reconnect with Your Soul"

Workshop Chapter 5: "Spiritual Rebirth – Breaking the Rules to Reconnect with Your Soul"

Introduction:

At some point in life, the rules you were told to follow—who to be, how to act, what to chase—stop making sense. You look around and realize you've been surviving, not *living*. That's when something inside you shifts.

You don't need a breakdown, you need a **rebirth**.

Spiritual rebirth happens when you **break free from who the world told you to be** and start listening to the quiet voice within your soul.

🌱 What Is Spiritual Rebirth?

It's not about religion. It's about awakening.
It's when you:

- Stop running from your past and start **learning from it.**
- Let go of people, patterns, and beliefs that **no longer serve you.**
- Begin a personal quest to **reclaim your power**, **your destiny**, and **your truth.**

It's not becoming someone new, it's remembering who you were before the world changed you.

⚙️ Starting the Personal Quest

To reconnect with your soul and rediscover your life's purpose, you must:

1. **Be still** – Silence is the soul's native language.
2. **Reflect honestly** – What parts of yourself have you been denying?
3. **Let go** – Release old identities built on pain, fear, or approval-seeking.
4. **Listen inward** – Your intuition knows the way. Trust it.
5. **Follow the pull** – What lights your spirit up, even if it makes no "logical" sense?

🔥 Breaching the Rules of Life

- You don't have to stay in survival mode.
- You don't need anyone's permission to start over.
- You are not your trauma, your title, or your mistakes.

You were born with purpose, even if the world taught you to forget it.

📝 Workshop Exercise: Soul Reconnection Journal

1. Write 3 things you used to love as a child before life got loud.
2. Write 2 beliefs that keep you from fully stepping into your purpose.
3. Write 1 bold step you can take this week to move closer to your true calling.

✨ Affirmation:

"I am not lost—I am being reborn. I release who I had to be and welcome who I am becoming."

🪟 Closing Thought:

Spiritual rebirth isn't about perfection. It's about permission—**to live, to feel, to grow, to change.** You break the rules not to rebel, but to return— to your soul, your power, and your purpose.

"The most powerful journey you'll ever take is the one that leads you back to yourself."

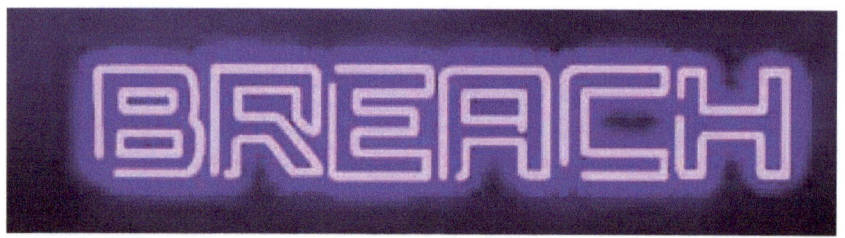

For you could belittle truth or deny its existence, but the truth will always be there, regardless of lack of understanding, disbelief, or ignorance.

the Weekly
JOURNAL

Workshop Chapter 6: "Self-Development – From Hookups to Healing: Building Real Love by Knowing Yourself"

Workshop Chapter 6: "Self-Development – From Hookups to Healing: Building Real Love by Knowing Yourself"

Introduction:

In a world that rewards surface-level attraction and quick pleasure, it's easy to confuse attention for connection. We've all broken the rules, chased lust over love, used people to fill voids, or avoided commitment to protect our hearts. But there comes a moment when those patterns no longer feel empowering... they feel **empty**.

That's where **self-development** comes in.
Not to be perfect, but to become **authentically connected to yourself**, so that you can build something real—with someone who sees you, not just your body.

🧠 What Self-Development Truly Means

Self-development isn't just reading books or setting goals about:

- Healing the wounds that keep you choosing *temporary* over *true*.
- Becoming emotionally available for the kind of love you desire.
- Building the courage to say: *"I'm done performing. I want something real."*

The journey to real love begins with real self-love.

💡 Breaking the Rules of the Hook-Up Culture

Society says:

- "Stay casual feelings make things messy."
- "Play the game—don't catch feelings."
- "You can't be lonely if you're never alone."

But the truth is:

- Emotional intimacy **requires vulnerability.**
- Authentic connection **requires clarity.**
- Long-term relationships **require self-work.**

You can't build a deep connection on shallow ground.

 Essential Tools for Real Connection

1. **Self-Awareness**
   Know your patterns. Why do you chase what doesn't last?
2. **Emotional Regulation**
   Learn to respond, not react. Love can't grow in chaos.
3. **Communication Skills**
   Be open about your needs and honest about your fears.
4. **Boundaries with Intention**
   Stop entertaining what doesn't align with your long-term values.
5. **Vulnerability**
   Let someone *see* you—not just touch you.

 Workshop Exercise: From Casual to Committed

1. Write 3 traits you admire in the kind of relationship you desire.
2. Reflect: Have your recent choices aligned with those traits?

3. Write one action step to shift away from temporary situations and toward intentional connection.

Example:
💔 Pattern: "Late-night DMs & meaningless flings"
➡️ Shift: "Unfollow distractions. Start conversations with purpose."

✨ **Affirmation:**

"I am worthy of a love that matches my growth. I no longer shrink to fit into situations that weren't built to last."

⚪ **Closing Thought:**

Real love doesn't start with swipes. It starts with **self-awareness**. When you know who you are, you are attracted to who aligns with you. When you love yourself deeply, you refuse to settle for shallow connections. Break the rule that says love must hurt or be a game.

"Your soul deserves more than your body has been settling for."

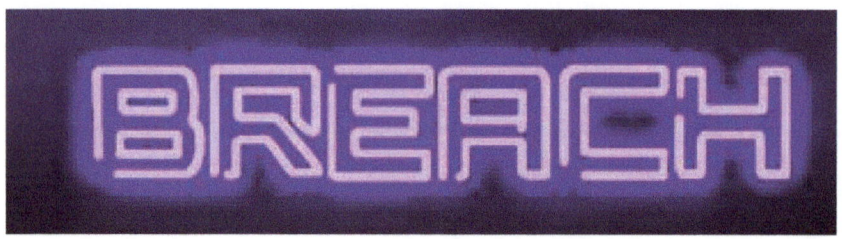

You have learned to trust your senses in what you can taste, smell, touch, see, and hear. While sense perception is great in life experience, it limits you when it comes to expanding your spiritual awareness. At one time, you had to count on your sense of intuition and inner knowing. But now we simply lose touch due to modern technology.

In my opinion, everyone has a Superpower. It is your Intuition Chakras. The power to be able to trust your gut. To pay attention to a hunch or a subtle feeling of moving forward or holding back. Trust that feeling of intuition to stay true to yourself. That is your power. Remember your enemy power is manipulation and the art of persuasion. And if you ever find yourself in a conflict, ask for your sense of intuition to be opened to you to help give your mind the clarity it needs to make the right choice.

the Weekly
JOURNAL

Workshop Chapter 7: "Self-Worth – Breaking the Rules to Fully Love Yourself"

Workshop Chapter 7: "Self-Worth – Breaking the Rules to Fully Love Yourself"

Introduction:

For most of our lives, we're taught to measure our worth by **outside validation**—who loves us, who chooses us, what we look like, or what we achieve. But chasing worth from the world leaves you in a constant state of performing, pleasing, and proving.

Self-worth begins when you break that cycle.
It begins when you realize: *I don't need to be more to be enough.*

🔴 Breaching the Rules of False Worth

Society says:

- "Be perfect to be loved."
- "Your value is tied to your looks, success, or relationship status."
- "Don't be too much. Don't take up too much space."

But here's the truth:

- **Perfection is an illusion.**
- **You were born worthy.**
- **Loving yourself isn't arrogance, it's survival.**

🌱 What Real Self-Worth Looks Like

- You **accept your flaws** without apology.
- You don't chase love—you **attract it by honoring yourself.**
- You make **decisions based on your truth**, not your fear.

Self-worth is quiet but powerful. It doesn't need to scream. It **chooses peace** over performance.

💬 Signs You're Still Seeking Worth Outside Yourself

- You change who you are to fit in.
- You over-give to be accepted.
- You tolerate disrespect because "something is better than nothing."
- You only feel "enough" when someone validates you.

🛠️ How to Build Unshakable Self-Worth

1. **Affirm the Truth** – Every day, say something kind to yourself that isn't based on what you've done, but *who you are.*
2. **Break Toxic Agreements** – Let go of the belief that you're "too broken," "too loud," or "not enough."
3. **Treat Yourself Like Someone You Love** – Speak to yourself with grace, protect your energy, and honor your boundaries.
4. **Choose You—Loudly** – Even when it's hard. Especially when it's lonely.

📝 Workshop Exercise: The Worth Mirror

Stand in front of a mirror and say (even if it feels uncomfortable):

- "I am enough, right now."
- "I forgive myself for the ways I abandoned my own worth."
- "I choose to see myself through loving eyes."

Now journal:

- What am I proud of about myself?
- What part of me deserves more love and attention?
- What would life look like if I stopped chasing approval?

✨ Affirmation:

"I no longer beg for love or shrink for comfort. I was born enough. And today, I choose to believe it."

💬 Closing Thought:

Self-worth isn't something you earn. It's something you remember. Break the rule that says love must come from others first. Let it come from **you**. Let it **rise in you, anchor in you**, and lead every step you take from here forward.

"You are not a half waiting to be made whole. You are already complete."

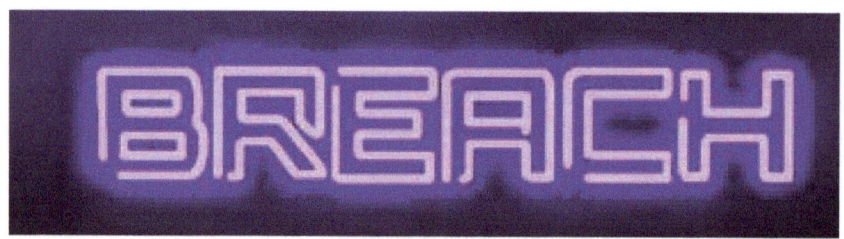

Be honest. Be clear about your intentions from the start. Basically, you have set the goal of wanting to meet your dream partner, but you also must surrender it back to the universe so that you can allow it to supply the best partner for you.

the Weekly
JOURNAL

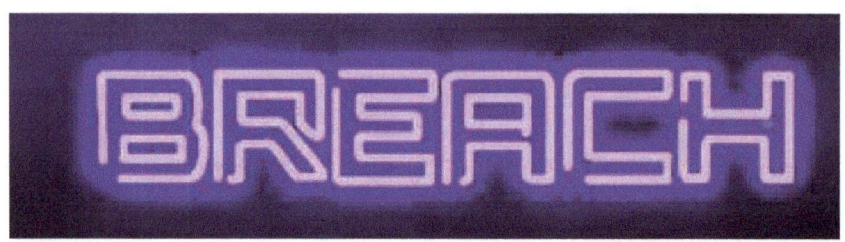

When you know your worth. You move differently. Do not let anyone treat you like you are average. You get what you settle for, so aim high and surround yourself with those who see your self-worth, who love you, who respect you, who encourage you and build you up to a higher level. You are special, and you can achieve anything, remember that.

the Weekly
JOURNAL

Workshop Chapter 8: "Love Blocks – Breaking the Rules to Let Love In"

Workshop Chapter 8: "Love Blocks – Breaking the Rules to Let Love In"

Introduction:

We all want love—but many of us carry invisible walls around our hearts. Not because we're broken, but because somewhere along the way, we were taught that love had to be earned, performed for, or controlled. These "rules of life" were meant to protect us—but they end up blocking the very connection we crave.

Real love begins when you stop following rules that teach you to guard your heart instead of opening it.

● **The Rules That Block Love**

Society says:

- "Don't be too vulnerable—it's weakness."
- "If you want love, make yourself easy to love."
- "Family is love, no matter how it hurts."
- "You have to prove you're worthy of affection."

But here's the truth:

- Vulnerability is your strength.
- Real love accepts the real you.
- Not all love is healthy—and it's okay to walk away.
- You don't have to *earn* love. You *are* love.

🌱 How Breaking These Rules Heals Your Heart

When You're Single:

- You stop chasing unavailable people.
- You release shame around wanting love.
- You realize that your loneliness doesn't mean you're unlovable, it means you're clearing space for real connection.

In a Relationship:

- You stop pretending everything's fine when it's not.
- You express your needs without fear of being "too much."
- You no longer confuse attachment with love.

With Family:

- You recognize emotional abuse, even if it's normalized.
- You give yourself permission to take space.
- You learn to reparent yourself when love was conditional growing up.

💬 Signs You're Carrying Love Blocks

- You push people away when they get too close.
- You hide your true feelings to keep the peace.
- You don't trust people who show you real kindness.
- You believe love must be earned through sacrifice or silence.

🛠 How to Let Love In

1. **Identify the Rules You Inherited**
   (e.g., "I'm not lovable unless I'm useful.")
2. **Challenge the Lie**
   Ask: *Is this belief helping me feel loved—or just keeping me safe from hurt?*
3. **Make Love a Safe Place Again**
   Surround yourself with people who don't require you to shrink.
4. **Choose to Be Seen**
   Every time you let someone witness your truth, you make space for real love.

📝 **Workshop Exercise: Clearing the Heart Gate**

Part 1: Journal Prompt

- What message did I grow up believing about love?
- What rule about love has kept me in fear?
- What would it look like to *trust* love again?

Part 2: Mirror Practice
Stand in front of a mirror and say:

- "I am worthy of real, healthy love."
- "I let go of love that required me to abandon myself."
- "I open my heart to be seen, valued, and met."

✦ **Affirmation:**

"I   do   not   chase,   beg,   or   perform   for   love.
I   break   every   rule   that   told   me   I   had   to.
I am love. And I am safe to receive it."

💬 Closing Thought:

Love is not a prize for the perfect.
It's a birthright for honesty, healing, and the whole.
The moment you break the rules that kept your heart behind bars, you realize love isn't locked outside, it's been waiting inside you all along.

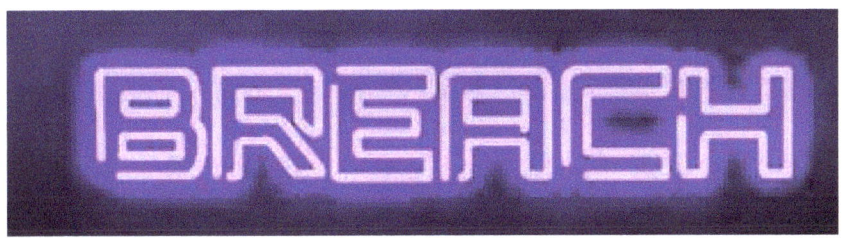

Your unresolved emotional baggage could hold you back from finding true love. Remember, the most difficult part of self-realization is taking responsibility rather than placing blame. Remember, you are the only person responsible for your emotions. They belong to you, and you are alone. Own them, and take responsibility for how you feel, and every single one of your relationships will benefit from it – particularly the one you have with yourself.

the Weekly
JOURNAL

Workshop Chapter 9: "Holistic Connection – Breaking the Rules to Feel Fully Seen"

Workshop Chapter 9: "Holistic Connection – Breaking the Rules to Feel Fully Seen"

Introduction:

Connection is a basic human need—but many of us feel unseen, unheard, or misunderstood. Why? Because society teaches us to connect through roles, appearances, or surface-level interaction—not through truth.

Real connection doesn't come from fitting in. It comes from showing up fully—even if that breaks a few rules.

Holistic connection means being emotionally, mentally, and spiritually present—with yourself and with others. And that begins with breaking the habits that tell you to hide.

🔴 **Rules That Block True Connection**

Society says:

- "Don't be too honest—it'll scare people away."
- "Stay in your role: the strong one, the smart one, the caregiver."
- "Keep it light—nobody wants to hear about your struggles."
- "Connection means being agreeable, not authentic."

But here's the truth:

- Vulnerability is magnetic.
- You are more than a role—you're a whole person.
- Sharing your struggle builds trust.
- Real connection starts where pretending ends.

🌱 How Holistic Connection Heals in Every Season

When You're Single:

- You deepen your self-awareness without rushing into distraction.
- You build friendships that nourish, not just fill time.
- You create a sacred connection with yourself—through solitude, stillness, and truth.

In a Relationship:

- You move from performance to partnership.
- You stop assuming and start communicating.
- You recognize emotional intimacy as just as important as physical closeness.

With Family:

- You shift from obligation to honesty.
- You release roles and reveal who you really are.
- You connect not out of guilt, but out of genuine love.

🧠 Signs You're Craving Holistic Connection

- You feel lonely even in company.
- You hide parts of yourself to be accepted.
- You long for "real" conversations.
- You miss *you*—because you're not fully showing up.

🛠️ Steps to Build Holistic Connection

1. **Unmask Yourself Gently**
   Share one truth with someone close to you, something real and vulnerable.
2. **Practice Presence**
   Put down the phone, look into someone's eyes, and truly listen.
3. **Reclaim Rituals**
   Make space for deep connection—weekly check-ins, family truth circles, journaling, or solo reflection.
4. **Define Connection for Yourself**
   Ask: *What does being fully connected feel like to me?*

📝 Workshop Exercise: The Connection Compass

Part 1: Journal Prompts

- Where in my life am I faking connection?
- What part of me have I been hiding from others?
- What would change if I brought my full self into the room?

Part 2: Connection Practice
With a trusted person (or in the mirror), say:

- "This is who I am beyond what I do."
- "I want connection that sees all of me—not just what's easy."
- "I invite truth and depth into my relationships."

✦ Affirmation:

"I break every rule that asked me to perform connection instead of feel it. I choose truth over comfort.
I connect deeply—with myself, with others, and with life."

Closing Thought:

Holistic connection is a radical act in a world of surface-level attention. When you stop pretending and start *presenting*—fully, honestly, soulfully—you'll find that the love you longed for was never missing. It just needed the *real you* to show up.

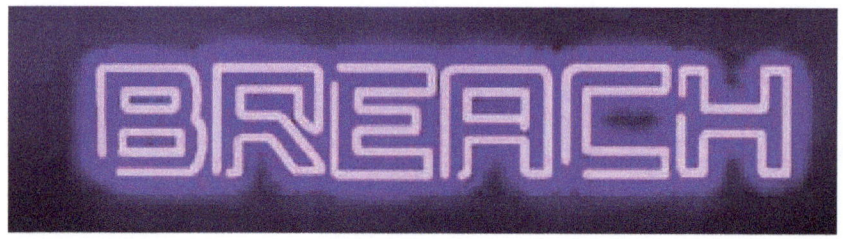

"Being vulnerable with your partner can seem scary but doing so is quite valuable for fostering and maintaining a sense of intimacy. This question is important because so many couples avoid difficult subjects, and resentment builds.

the Weekly JOURNAL

Workshop Chapter 10: "Dating Rules – Breaking the Patterns That Block Real Love"

Workshop Chapter 10: "Dating Rules – Breaking the Patterns That Block Real Love"

Introduction:

From rom coms to family advice, most of us grew up hearing "rules" about how to date: Don't call first. Play hard to get. Settle down by a certain age. Be attractive but not too assertive.

These rules may have been meant to protect us—but they often teach us to perform, manipulate, or hide.

Real love doesn't follow scripts—it responds to truth.

Dating should never cost your self-worth, your identity, or your peace. To find authentic connection, you sometimes have to break the rules.

🔴 Dating Rules That Keep You Disconnected

Society says:

- "Don't be too available."
- "You need to 'fix' yourself before you're lovable."
- "You're too picky if you want emotional depth."
- "Your family/age/background determines your value."

But here's the truth:

- Availability is strength, not weakness.
- You are not a project, you are a person, worthy now.
- Depth isn't too much; it's necessary.
- Love is not earned through perfection—it's attracted through presence.

🌱 How Breaking Dating Rules Creates Real Connection

When You're Single:

- You stop performing to "catch" someone and start showing up as yourself.
- You embrace this season as self-discovery, not a waiting room.
- You release pressure and invite possibility.

In a Relationship:

- You stop following toxic advice like "don't rock the boat."
- You speak your truth and invite deeper intimacy.
- You stop settling for patterns that mimic love but lack depth.

With Family Influence:

- You let go of generational fears around love and relationships.
- You choose love that reflects your truth—not your upbringing's approval.
- You set boundaries with loved ones who push outdated views of who you should date.

🗨 Signs You're Still Living by Limiting Dating Rules

- You hide your real intentions to appear "cool."
- You avoid expressing emotions out of fear of rejection.
- You measure your worth by attention, not alignment.
- You feel pressure to be in a relationship just to be "valid."

🛠️ How to Date Without Losing Yourself

1. **Unlearn, Then Relearn**
   Ask yourself: *Is this rule helping me love better—or just fear better?*

2. **Center Your Emotional Safety**
   Stop choosing chemistry over consistency. Prioritize how people make you feel, not how they make you chase.

3. **Be Clear, Not Careful**
   You can express interest without losing power. You don't have to play games to earn real love.

4. **Redefine What a "Good Match" Means**
   Choose alignment, not perfection. A good match won't ask you to abandon yourself.

📝 Workshop Exercise: Rewrite Your Dating Rulebook

Part 1: Journal Prompts

- What dating "rule" has kept me hiding my real self?
- How have my family's beliefs shaped my dating expectations?
- What would dating look like if I approached it with curiosity, not control?

Part 2: Heart Reframe
Write one outdated dating rule you've followed. Then rewrite it into a truth that honors your self-worth.

Example:
Old Rule: "Don't call first—you'll seem desperate."
New Truth: "I initiate when I feel moved to connect. That's strength, not weakness."

✦ Affirmation:

"I don't date to perform.
I don't chase to prove.
I break every rule that asked me to be less to be loved.
I show up whole, honest, and free."

💬 Closing Thought:

Dating is not a test to pass or a game to win.
It's an invitation to be seen, to choose, and to connect with integrity.
When you break the rules that taught you to hide—
you create space for the kind of love that's not just romantic,
but *real*.

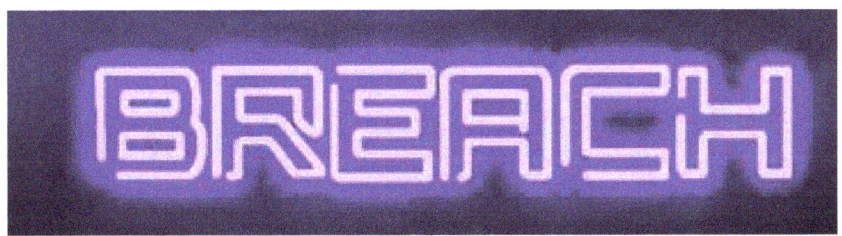

We live in a disconnected world. That your value is judge buy your photo on a dating app or physical looks. But everyone wants to be loved, not for their looks, race, background, or income. An emotional connection is key to a long-term marriage or relationship not physical attraction. You must form an intimate bond with the person. It is a big decision you must make in life. Ask yourself this question? Is love truly blind? Will the physical attraction of the person and your sexual urges sabotage a real connection with someone?

the Weekly
JOURNAL

Workshop Chapter 11: "Healing Your Inner Child – Breaking the Rules to Love the Parts You Hid"

Workshop Chapter 11: "Healing Your Inner Child – Breaking the Rules to Love the Parts You Hid"

Introduction:

Inside every adult is a younger self still craving safety, love, and attention. Many of us were taught to silence that voice, "grow up," and bury our needs in order to survive. But true healing doesn't mean ignoring your inner child means going back and giving them what they never got.

Healing your inner child is an act of rebellion—and restoration. It breaks the rules that tell you your emotions were too much.

🔴 **Rules That Silenced Your Inner Child**

Growing up, you may have heard:

- "Stop crying or I'll give you something to cry about."
- "You're too sensitive."
- "Be strong. Be quiet. Be good."
- "What happens in this house, stays in this house."

But here's the truth:

- Emotions are not weaknesses.
- Sensitivity is not a flaw—it's a superpower.
- You are allowed to revisit pain to repair your peace.
- Speaking your truth isn't betrayal, it's healing.

🌱 **How Inner Child Healing Impacts Your Present Life**

When You're Single:

- You stop seeking others to "fix" what's unhealed.
- You learn to parent yourself with patience and compassion.
- You attract love from wholeness, not wounds.

In a Relationship:

- You stop expecting your partner to meet unmet childhood needs.
- You recognize emotional triggers as invitations to heal.
- You learn to communicate with maturity—not through tantrums or shutdowns.

With Family:

- You break generational trauma cycles with awareness and boundaries.
- You release guilt for choosing healing over silence.
- You allow your truth to take up space, even if it wasn't welcomed growing up.

🧠 Signs Your Inner Child Is Calling Out

- You feel overly hurt by criticism or rejection.
- You people-please feel safe or accepted.
- You shut down emotionally when conflict arises.
- You fear abandonment—even in stable relationships.

🛠 How to Begin Inner Child Healing

1. **Acknowledge Their Existence**
   You still carry that younger self. They deserve to be seen, not suppressed.
2. **Identify the Wounds**
   Ask: *What needs went unmet? What messages did I internalize that still hurt me today?*
3. **Reparent Yourself Daily**
   Offer words and care your caregivers never gave you. Start small but consistent.
4. **Protect Your Inner Child Like You Would a Real One**
   Don't put yourself in environments that recreate old wounds.

 Workshop Exercise: The Inner Child Letter

Part 1: Journal Prompts

- What age was I when I first felt unseen or unsafe?
- What did I need to hear back then?
- What parts of me still crave that love now?

Part 2: Write a Letter
Write a compassionate letter to your younger self. Start with:

"Dear younger me, I know you didn't feel safe/loved/seen. But I'm here now. You don't have to hide anymore…"

✦ Affirmation:

"I no longer ignore the child within me.
I see them, hear them, and love them fiercely.
I break the rules that told me to be quiet and strong.
I choose healing—loudly and unapologetically."

◯ Closing Thought:

Your inner child doesn't want perfection; they want presence. They want to know that someone is finally listening.

Healing isn't about erasing the past.
It's about holding space for the younger you and showing them:
We're safe now. We loved it. And we're free to be whole.

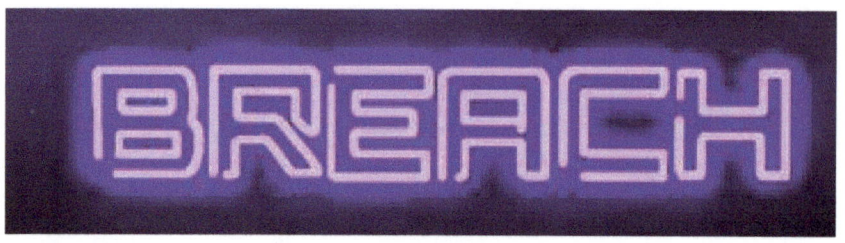

Healing your inner child means breaking the old, unspoken rules that tell you to hide your emotions, stay small, or be perfect — not the rules that protect your safety or others'. Love the parts of yourself you once buried, but do it with compassion, responsibility, and care for your healing journey and those around you."

the Weekly JOURNAL

Workshop Chapter 12: "Healing Old Wounds – Breaking the Rules to Finally Feel Free"

Workshop Chapter 12: "Healing Old Wounds – Breaking the Rules to Finally Feel Free"

Introduction:

Old wounds don't disappear with time—they hide in our habits, fears, and relationships. We're often taught to move on, stay strong, or suppress pain. But ignoring the wound doesn't heal it, it just teaches you how to live around it.

Healing begins when you stop pretending, you're over it and start giving your pain the space it deserves.

You don't need to stay strong for everyone. You need to be honest with yourself.

🔴 Rules That Block Healing

Society and upbringing say:

- "Time heals everything."
- "Don't talk about the past—just move forward."
- "Strong people don't cry over old stuff."
- "Forgive and forget, even if it still hurts."

But here's the truth:

- Time alone doesn't heal—intentional attention does.
- Talking about the past is how we take back our power.
- Tears don't mean weakness, they mean release.
- Forgiveness doesn't mean silence—and you don't owe access to people who hurt you.

🌱 How Healing Old Wounds Transforms Every Area of Life

When You're Single:

- You stop projecting pain onto potential partners.
- You date with clarity, not fear.
- You realize your wholeness doesn't come from someone else, it comes from healing what's already yours.

In a Relationship:

- You break cycles of mistrust, defensiveness, or shutdown.
- You stop expecting your partner to pay for wounds they didn't cause.
- You become capable of deeper intimacy—because you're not protecting old scars.

With Family:

- You create new boundaries without guilt.
- You speak truth to old pain—even if others deny it.
- You stop repeating generational hurt by healing it in you.

💬 Signs of Unhealed Wounds in Daily Life

- You overreact to small triggers.
- You push away love out of fear it will leave.
- You stay in relationships that feel familiar—but not safe.
- You feel stuck between wanting to heal and being afraid to face it.

🛠 How to Begin Healing Old Wounds

1. **Name the Pain**
   Healing starts with naming what hurt. Be specific. You're not too sensitive, you're aware.
2. **Break the Rule of Silence**
   You're allowed to talk about what hurt you—even if others wish you wouldn't.
3. **Stop Repeating the Wound**
   Notice when you're reliving old hurt in new situations. Ask: *Is this a reaction to now, or a memory of before?*
4. **Honor Your Healing Pace**
   You don't have to rush closure. You just have to be consistent with your care.

📝 Workshop Exercise: The Wound Reclamation

Part 1: Journal Prompts

- What's one wound I've been pretending doesn't hurt anymore?
- What would it feel like to speak about it without shame?
- How has this wound affected how I trust, love, or show up?

Part 2: Write a Truth Statement
Complete this sentence:

"The wound I am ready to stop hiding is ___. I may not be fully healed, but today I choose to care for it with love and truth.

✨ Affirmation:

"I no longer carry old wounds in silence.
I break the rules that told me to be quiet, tough, or forget.
I heal at my pace, with my truth, and in my own power.
I am not broken—I am becoming whole."

💬 **Closing Thought:**

You don't have to pretend it didn't hurt.
You don't have to carry it alone.

Healing your wounds doesn't make you weak.
It makes you *wise, powerful, and whole*.
Let this be the season where you stop hiding pain—and start rewriting your story.

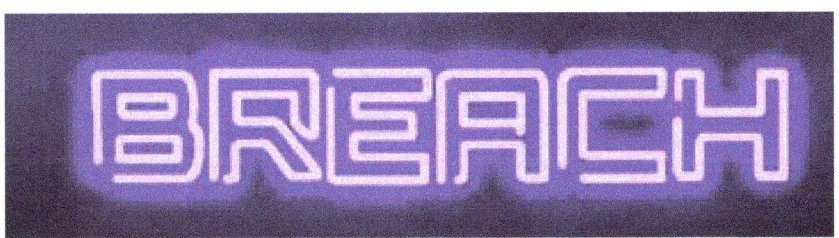

"Healing old wounds sometimes means breaking the rules that kept you silent, ashamed, or stuck — not the ones that keep you and others safe. True freedom comes from rewriting the inner scripts that no longer serve you, with honesty, courage, and care.

the Weekly
JOURNAL

Workshop Chapter 13: "Your Gift, Your Purpose – Breaking the Rules to Fully Become Who You Are"

Workshop Chapter 13: "Your Gift, Your Purpose – Breaking the Rules to Fully Become Who You Are"

Introduction:

We are all born with gifts—natural abilities, instincts, and callings that want to flow through us. But society teaches us to trade those gifts for approval, productivity, or perfection. We're told to follow the rules: play it safe, stay quiet, fit in.

Your gift doesn't serve the world when it's hidden. And your purpose doesn't wait for permission.

To step into your purpose, you must be willing to break the rules that tell you who you "should" be—and remember who you *are*.

⬤ Rules That Block You from Living in Your Purpose

The world says:

- "Play it safe dreams don't pay bills."
- "Be realistic. That's not a real job/talent/path."
- "Stay in your lane. Don't shine too bright."
- "You need to be chosen to matter."

But here's the truth:

- Playing it safe often means playing small.
- Your gift doesn't have to make sense to others, it's sacred to *you*.
- Playing dim won't make others shine brighter.
- You don't need to be chosen, you just need to show up.

How Purpose Aligns Your Whole Life

When You're Single:

- You stop defining your worth by your relationship status.
- You create joy, meaning, and momentum on your own terms.
- You realize: your life is not on pause, it's in power.

In a Relationship:

- You stop compromising your calling, to keep the peace.
- You invite your partner to witness your growth—not control it.
- You model what it means to love someone who's lit up from within.

With Family:

- You break the cycle of living out someone else's dream.
- You give future generations permission to follow their truth.
- You stop performing the role they expected and start living the truth you need.

Signs You're Abandoning Your Gift or Purpose

- You feel stuck doing what's "expected" but not what's fulfilling.
- You downplay your talents to make others comfortable.
- You wait for permission, credentials, or the "right time" to start.
- You feel guilty for wanting more out of life.

✹ How to Reclaim Your Gift and Purpose

1. **Get Honest About What Lights You Up**
   Stop asking what's practical. Ask: *What brings me alive?*
2. **Reframe the Fear of Being "Too Much"**
   You're not too much—you've just been around environments that were too small.
3. **Make Space to Practice Your Gift**
   You don't need to monetize it today—just honor it daily.
4. **Say Yes Before You're Ready**
   Purpose doesn't wait for perfection—it responds to presence.

📝 Workshop Exercise: Purpose Declaration

Part 1: Journal Prompts

- What's something I've always loved doing, even when no one was watching?
- What limiting belief has kept me from living in my gift?
- What would my life look like if I trusted that my purpose was enough?

Part 2: Write a Declaration
Start with:

"My gift is ___. I don't need to be approved or validated to use it. I will no longer shrink. I was born for this."

✦ Affirmation:

"I break the rules that told me to be quiet, safe, or small.
I honor my gifts, even if they scare others.
I am no longer waiting—I am walking in purpose now."

Closing Thought:

You don't have to chase your purpose, it's already within you.
It's not about being famous, perfect, or busy.

It's about being *you*, fully and freely.
Let this be the season where your gift rises, unapologetically—
and your purpose finally leads.

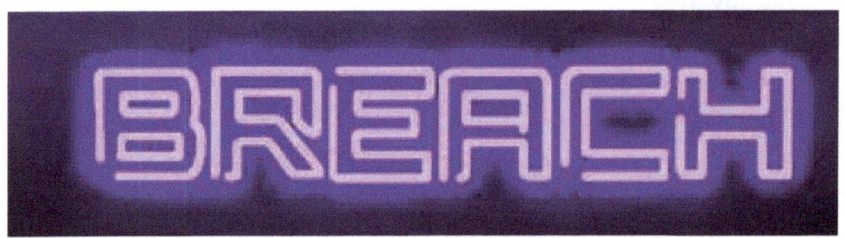

Becoming who you truly are may mean breaking the rules that tell you to play small, fit in, or follow someone else's path. These are the rules worth defying—so your gift can shine, and your purpose can lead. Break free, not harmfully, but truthfully."

the Weekly
JOURNAL

Workshop Chapter 16: "Emotional Connection – Breaking the Rules to Truly Feel and Be Felt"

Workshop Chapter 16: "Emotional Connection – Breaking the Rules to Truly Feel and Be Felt"

Introduction:

Emotional connection is one of the most powerful human needs. Yet so many people walk through life feeling unseen, unheard, and misunderstood. Why? Because we've been taught that emotions are inconvenient, weakness, or something to "get over."

Real connection starts when you stop managing emotions—and start meeting them.

When you give yourself permission to feel and express, you break the cycle of emotional silence that blocks intimacy.

🛑 **Rules That Block Emotional Connection**

Society and culture teach:

- "Don't talk about your feelings—it makes people uncomfortable."
- "Crying is weakness."
- "Stay strong. Don't fall apart."
- "Be logical, not emotional."

But here's the truth:

- Suppressing feelings doesn't make them disappear—it disconnects you from others.
- Strength isn't staying silent, it's being honest.
- Logic without emotional depth builds walls, not bridges.

- You don't need to be perfect to be worthy of being felt—you need to be real.

🌱 How Emotional Connection Heals and Deepens Your Life

When You're Single:

- You learn to witness and validate your own feelings instead of outsourcing them.
- You stop pretending you're fine when you're really lonely or grieving.
- You attract deeper friendships and love by first connecting deeply with *yourself*.

In a Relationship:

- You stop arguing to win and start communicating to understand.
- You show up vulnerably, not just physically.
- You shift from surface-level love to soul-level intimacy.

With Family:

- You stop playing roles (the strong one, the silent one, the peacemaker) and start sharing your truth.
- You model emotional honesty for others who were never taught how.
- You stop repeating cycles of emotional neglect by choosing connection over silence.

🧠 Signs You're Craving Emotional Connection

- You feel lonely even around people.

- You dismiss your own feelings or apologize for them.
- You avoid emotional conversations out of fear they'll go wrong.
- You want to connect—but don't know how to say what you feel.

🛠 How to Build Real Emotional Connection

1. **Stop Saying "I'm Fine" When You're Not**
   Replace it with the truth—even if it's uncomfortable.
2. **Name the Emotion, Not Just the Reaction**
   Instead of "I'm mad," try "I feel unimportant and ignored."
3. **Share Before You Shut Down**
   Don't wait until the feeling becomes a wall—speak while there's still softness.
4. **Listen to Feel, Not Fix**
   Connection isn't always about solving. It's about *seeing* and *being seen*.

📝 Workshop Exercise: Feeling & Sharing Map

Part 1: Journal Prompts

- What feeling have I been hiding or downplaying lately?
- Who do I feel emotionally disconnected from, and why?
- What emotion do I wish someone would hold space for in me?

Part 2: Connection Practice
Choose someone you trust. Say:

"I've been feeling ___. I don't need advice—I just want to be real with you."

If you're alone:
Sit with your feeling in front of a mirror. Speak it aloud to yourself.

"Right now, I feel ___. And that's okay."

✦ Affirmation:

"I am no longer afraid of feeling deeply.
I break every rule that taught me to hide my emotions.
My feelings are not too much—they are my truth.
I am safe to connect."

💬 Closing Thought:

Emotional connection doesn't start with perfect words, it starts with brave truth.
When you stop pretending and start *presenting* your heart,
you invite the kind of connection that heals, strengthens, and lasts.

You don't just deserve to be heard—you deserve to be *felt*.

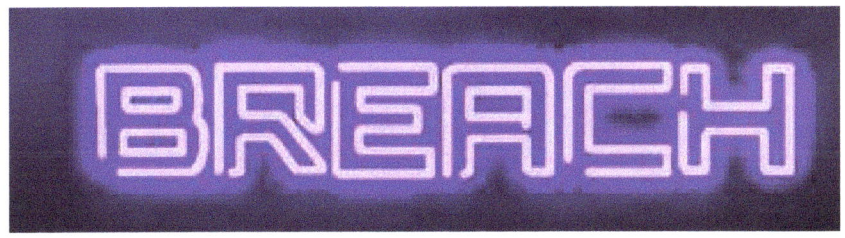

Real emotional connection begins when we break the old rules—don't cry, don't need, don't feel too much. To truly feel and be felt, we must risk vulnerability, speak truthfully, and stop hiding what makes us human."

:

the Weekly
JOURNAL

Workshop Chapter 11: "New Beginnings – Breaking the Rules to Start Again"

Workshop Chapter 11: "New Beginnings – Breaking the Rules to Start Again"

Introduction:

Starting over is often seen as failure like something went wrong, or like you "should've figured it out by now." But the truth is, **new beginnings are sacred.**
They're not signs of weakness; they're signs of courage, clarity, and self-trust.

To begin again, you have to let go of the rules that told you can't.

🔴 **Rules That Make New Beginnings Feel Wrong**

Society says:

- "You should have it all figured out by now."
- "Don't leave something stable for something uncertain."
- "Starting over means you failed."
- "You can't outgrow your family or your past."

But here's the truth:

- Growth is not linear.
- Sometimes walking away is wiser than staying stuck.
- You're allowed to outgrow people, places, and even parts of yourself.
- You don't need permission to begin again—you only need clarity.

🌱 Why New Beginnings Matter in Every Season

When You're Single:

- You stop waiting for life to begin "after" you find someone.
- You create purpose and joy on your terms.
- You shed shameful old stories and redefine who you are.

In a Relationship:

- You stop living in the past and co-create a fresh chapter.
- You end cycles of blame and invite new ways of loving.
- You choose presence over punishment—for yourself and your partner.

With Family:

- You forgive yourself for walking a different path.
- You stop living out inherited expectations.
- You allow your healing to begin—even if others don't understand it yet.

🧠 Signs You're Afraid to Begin Again

- You stay in situations that don't fit because they're familiar.
- You fear being judged for changing direction.
- You hold onto relationships out of guilt, not love.
- You postpone dreams waiting for "the right time."

🛠 How to Embrace a New Beginning

1. **Name the Ending**
   All new beginnings start with a brave goodbye. What do you need to let go of?
2. **Challenge the Timeline Rule**
   You are not behind. You're right on time for *your* life.
3. **Choose Wholeness, Not Approval**
   Start the chapter even if no one claps for you yet.
4. **Create a Ritual of Renewal**
   Light a candle. Write a letter. Say a prayer. Honor the moment you choose to begin again.

📝 **Workshop Exercise: The New Chapter Letter**

Part 1: Journal Prompts

- What old story about "starting over" do I need to release?
- What area of my life is asking for a fresh start?
- What would it look like if I trusted this new beginning?

Part 2: Write a letter to yourself
Start with:

"Dear me, I know starting over is scary, but this time, I choose..."

✦ **Affirmation:**

"I release the fear of starting again.
I break every rule that told me I had to stay the same.
I am not behind—I am becoming. And this new chapter belongs to me.

Closing Thought:

New beginnings are not signs of failure.
They are signs of *freedom.*
When you stop asking for permission to evolve,
you open doors to a life that reflects your truth.
No matter what your past, you're allowed to begin again—boldly,
beautifully, and without apology.

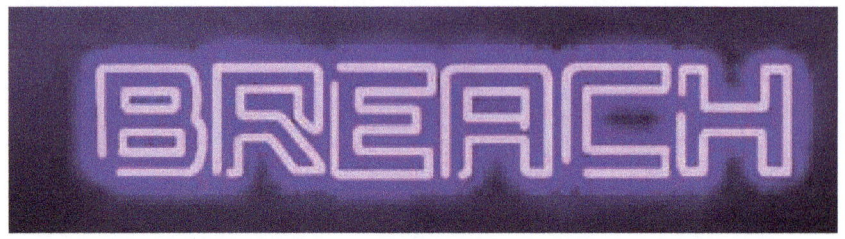

"Your inner child is waiting for a genuine, heartfelt apology." "The more you don't want to be like your parents, the more you will resemble them." "Healing is never complete until we have been truly heard. May the universe send you someone who will sincerely care to listen."

the Weekly
JOURNAL